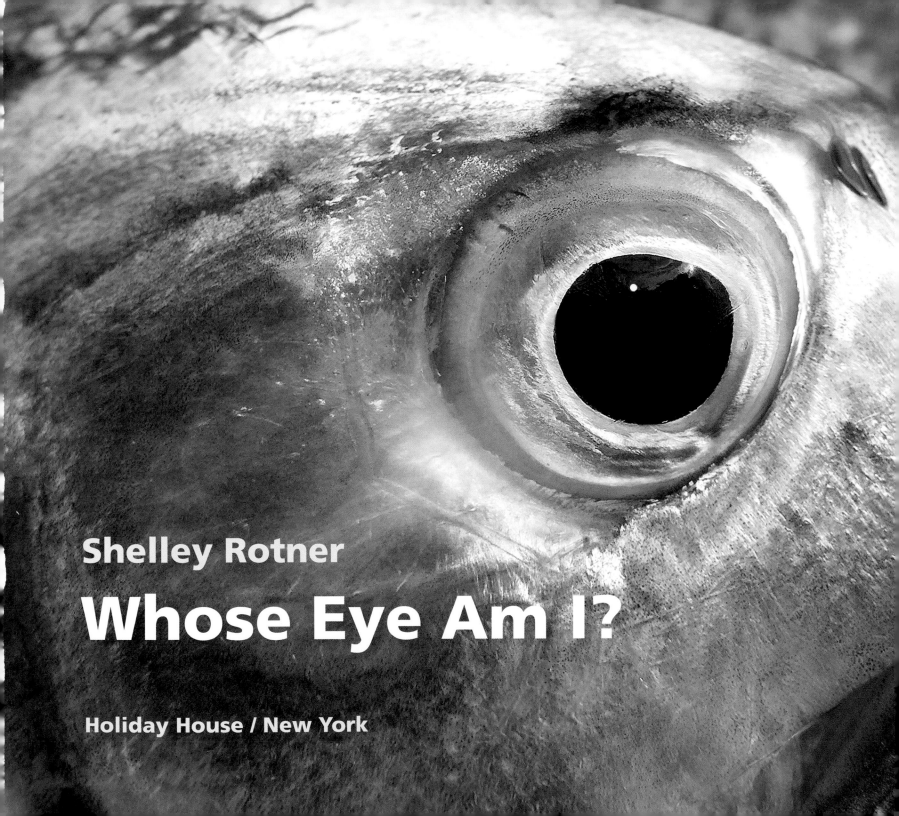

Shelley Rotner

Whose Eye Am I?

Holiday House / New York

We use our eyes to see the world.

So do other animals.

Eyes help us to see shapes, colors and movement.

Eyes tell us how big or small something is and how close to or far away from us it is.

Most animals need eyes to survive. Animals watch for danger with their eyes. They also use their eyes to find food and shelter.

Eyes help animals find mates and protect and raise their young.

Each animal has its own special way of seeing.

Scientists have learned much about how animals see.

Who am I?

A Dog

Dogs are very good at seeing motion. They see colors but not as many colors as humans can see. They don't see the color green. To dogs, green looks like yellow. Puppies are born blind and begin to see when they're a couple of weeks old.

Goats see well at night. Their *pupils* are wide, rectangular slits that let in lots of light and allow goats to see all around without moving.

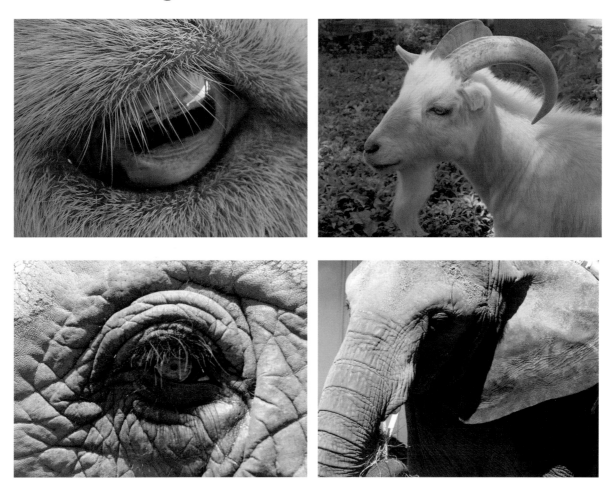

Elephants see better in dim light than in bright daylight. Their long *eyelashes* protect their eyes from blowing sand and dirt. When they are sad, they actually cry tears.

Giraffes are the tallest mammals and have sharp eyesight. Their height helps them spot predators.

Zebras have excellent eyesight, as well as good night vision. Because their eyes are on either side of their heads, they can see right and left at the same time.

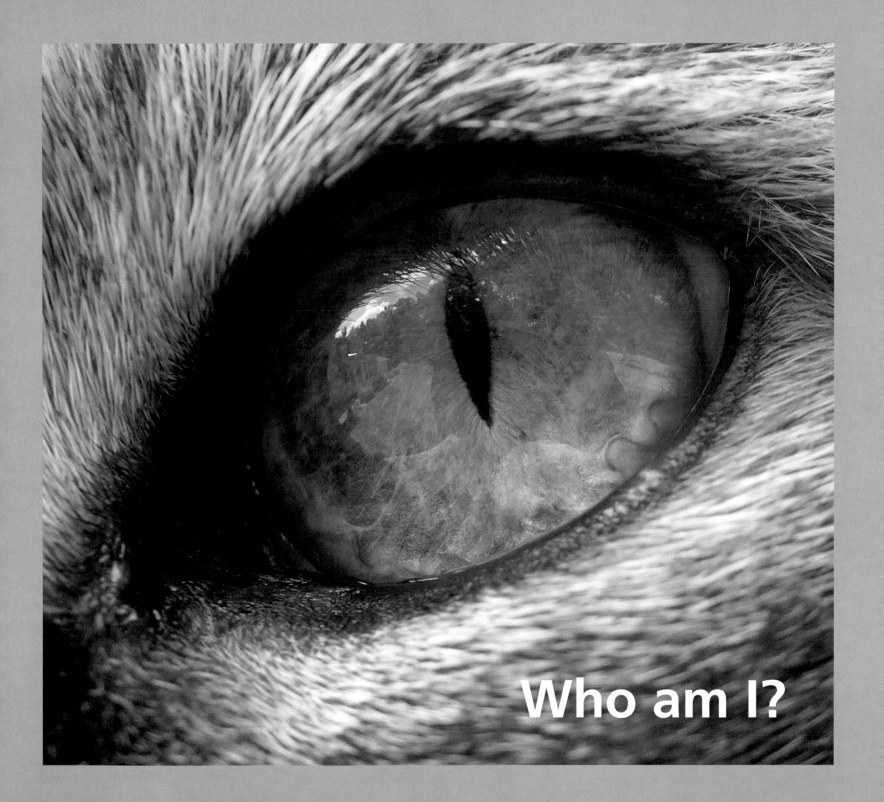

Who am I?

A Cat

Cats have better night vision than either humans or dogs. Their *pupils* can open wide to let in lots of light. Some experts believe that in the daytime, cats see everything in shades of blue and gray. Others believe their vision is similar to dogs but not as clear.

Who am I?

An Owl

Owls have the best night vision of any bird. Their eyes are the same size as human eyes even though they are much smaller animals. They can't move their eyes, but they can swivel their heads almost all the way around. Owls have third *eyelids* that clean and protect their eyes.

Birds, such as parrots, see millions of different colors, including colors that humans can't see at all. They probably have the best color range of any animal.

Pigeons have better color vision than almost any animal. They see colors that are invisible to humans. Sometimes they're used in search-and-rescue missions.

Swans have sharp eyesight, which they need for migrating. They fly higher than most birds when they are on the move.

Chickens can detect motion well, which helps them find tasty worms, bugs, toads and even snakes. They have third, see-through *eyelids* that protect their eyes from dirt.

Who am I?

A Frog

Frogs have eyes on top of their heads. Even when most of a frog's body is underwater it can see all around without moving, so it doesn't scare away prey. Frogs can see far away, even at night.

Who am I?

An Alligator

Alligators can see in dim light and for long distances. Clear third *eyelids* allow them to see well underwater. Their eyes are on top of their heads, which allows them to see even when they're mostly submerged underwater.

Snakes can't open or close their eyes. Their *eyelids* are clear covers. When a snake sheds its skin, it sheds its eyelids too.

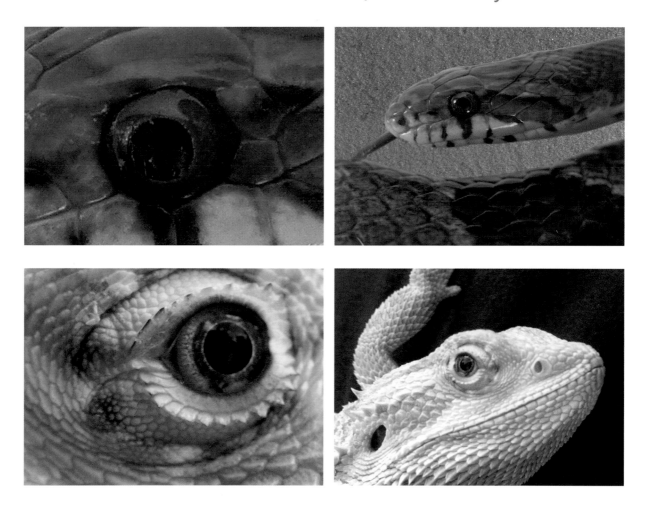

Bearded dragons see in full color and can see some colors that are invisible to us. Their eyes are on either side of their heads, so they see on both sides at once.

Turtles have good eyesight and can move their eyes around. They can see even more by stretching their long necks in different directions.

Chameleons can move each eye separately to see in different directions at the same time. Their *eyelids* cover almost the entire eyeball except for a small hole in the center.

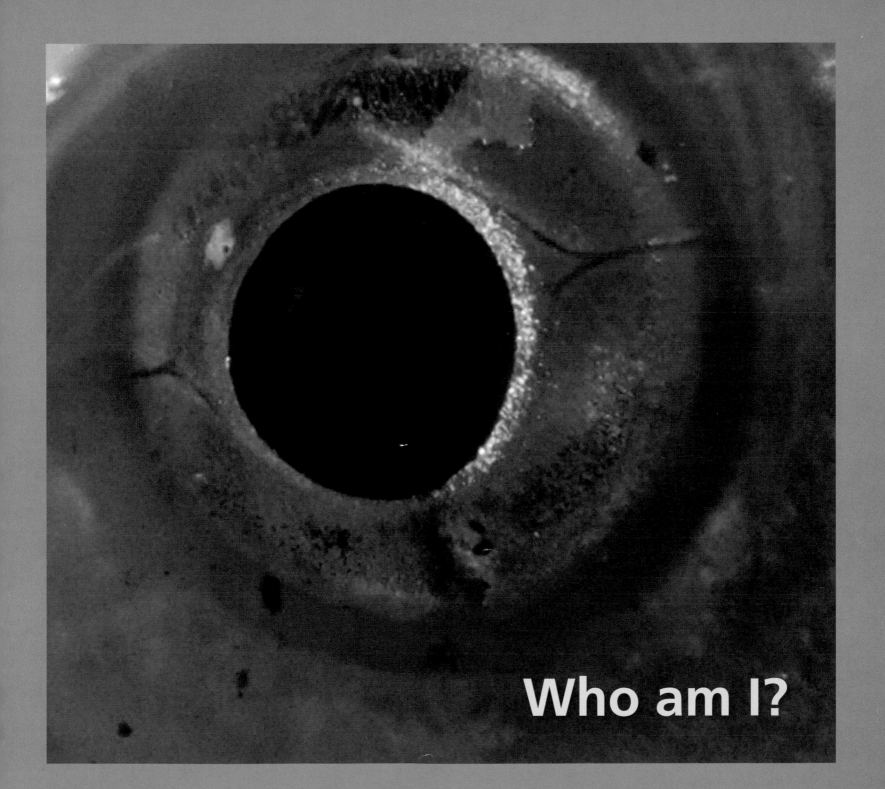

Who am I?

A Fish

Goldfish are the most researched of any fish and have been trained to recognize and react to various colors, including colors that are invisible to humans. They have no *eyelids* and sleep with their eyes open.

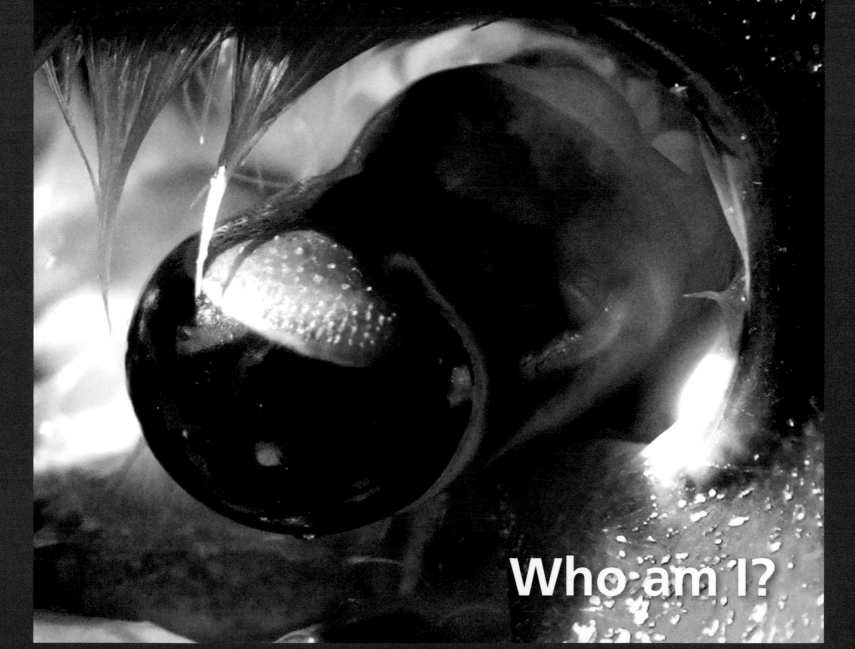

Who am I?

A Lobster

Lobsters have eyes at the base of their antennae. They can't see clear images but can detect movement well underwater and in the dark. Their eyes have thousands of *lenses* that reflect light. Their vision is so unusual, scientists have imitated it to make X-ray devices.

A **scallop** has up to a hundred eyes around the edge of its shell. Each one of these eyes reflects light like a mirror. Scallops cannot see shapes but respond to light and darkness.

Hermit crabs have eyes mounted on the tips of two stalks. By moving these stalks they can see in many different directions. They can see at night, but the images are not very sharp.

Starfish have an eye on the end of each of their arms to see forms, but not details.

Most spiders have eight eyes, but they still can't see very well. Some are nearly blind.

Beetles have two eyes on top of their heads that help them see movement and colors.

Tarantulas have eight eyes: two large round eyes in the middle and three on each side.

Who am I?

A Dragonfly

Dragonflies' eyes are huge compared to their body size and cover almost their entire head. They also have three smaller eyes that help detect motion. Their vision is excellent, and they can see colors that are invisible to humans.

Butterflies have large round eyes that detect motion well. Humans have one *lens* in each eye, but butterflies have thousands of lenses. They see colors humans can't see.

Bees have eyes made of thousands of small *lenses*. They see colors that are invisible to humans. This makes it easier to spot patterns on the petals of flowers that have the best nectar.

How Humans See

Humans see because of the way our eyes can process light.

Light goes through the **cornea** first, the clear surface that covers the front of the eye, and then travels through the dark opening in the

center called the **pupil**. The pupil is in the center of the **iris**, the colored part of the eye. The iris controls the size of the pupil. The pupil is small when light is bright but gets larger to let in more light when it is dark. Behind the iris is a **lens** that changes shape to focus the light. The shape of the lens depends on a number of things, including whether an object is close or farther away. After moving through the lens, the light reaches the back of the eye called the **retina**. At this point, the information is upside down and backward. The **optic nerve** sends what you see to your brain, where it is reversed and turned right side up.

Glossary

Cornea: the clear covering over the eye.

Eyelashes: the hairs along the upper and lower edges of your eyes that protect your eyes from dirt, dust and foreign materials.

Eyelids: the pieces of skin that cover your eyes when they are closed, or when you blink or squint. They protect your eyes from dirt, dust and bright light. They help spread tears to keep the eye moist.

Iris: the colored part of your eye that controls how much light is let into the eye.

Lens: the clear part of the eye that focuses light to form images.

Optic nerve: the nerve that sends images to the brain from the back of the eye.

Pupil: the opening in the eye that lets in light.

Retina: the back of the eyeball that has cells that are sensitive to light.

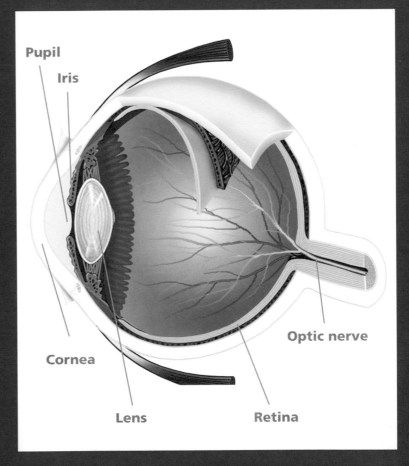

Index

Italicized page numbers indicate images.

alligator, *17, 18, 18*

bearded dragon, 19, *19*

bee, *3,* 29, *29*

beetle, 26, *26*

bird, *3, 4, 11,* 12, *12,* 13, *13,* 14, *14*

butterfly, *4,* 29, *29*

cat, *2, 3, 9,* 10, *10*

chameleon, 20, *20*

chicken, 14, *14*

color, 2, 6, 10, 13, 19, 22, 26, 28, 29

cornea, 30, 31, *31*

crab (hermit), 25, *25*

dog, 6, *6,* 10

dragonfly, 28, *28*

elephant, 7, *7*

eyelash, 7, 31, *31*

eyelid, 12, 14, 18, 19, 20, 22, 31

fish, *1, 21,* 22, *22*

frog, *15,* 16, *16*

giraffe, 8, *8*

goat, 7, *7*

human, *2,* 6, 10, 12, 13, 30, *30,* 31, *31*

insect, *3, 4,* 14, 26, *26, 27,* 28, *28,* 29, *29*

iris, 30, 31, *31*

lens, 24, 29, 30, 31, *31*

light, 7, 10, 24, 25, 30, 31

lizard, 19, *19,* 20, *20*

lobster, 24, *24*

motion detection, 2, 6, 14, 24, 26, 28, 29

night vision, 7, 8, 10, 12, 16, 25

optic nerve, 30, 31, *31*

owl, *11,* 12 , *12*

parrot, 13, *13*

pigeon, 13, *13*

predator, 8

prey, 16

pupil, 7, 10, 30, 31, *31*

retina, 30, 31, *31*

scallop, 25, *25*

snake, 14, 19, *19*

spider, 26, *26*

starfish, 26, *26*

swan, *3,* 14, *14*

tarantula, 26, *26*

turtle, 20, *20*

underwater vision, 18, 22, 24, 25

zebra, 8, *8*

Dedicated to my dad, who taught me how to see

Special thanks to Hobe Nature Center, Lion Country Safari, Diane deGroat and my designer, Hans Teensma.

Printed and Bound in November 2015 at Toppan Leefung, DongGuan City, China.
www.holidayhouse.com
First Edition
10 9 8 7 6 5 4 3 2 1

Library of Congress Cataloging-in-Publication Data
Rotner, Shelley, author, illustrator.
Whose eye am I? / Shelley Rotner. — First edition.
pages cm
  Audience: Ages 4-8.
  Audience: K to grade 3.
  Summary: "This introduction to how humans and other animals see also includes an interactive game in which readers guess which eye belongs to which animal."—Provided by publisher.
ISBN 978-0-8234-3558-6 (hardcover)
1. Eye—Juvenile literature. 2. Vision—Juvenile literature. 3. Anatomy—Juvenile literature. I. Title.
QP475.7.R68 2016
573.8'8—dc23
2015021764